WALKING
to COLD
MOUNTAIN

WALKING *to* COLD MOUNTAIN

A Journey Through Civil War America

C ARL Z EBROWSKI

Foreword by Ken Burns

SMITHMARK

This edition published in 1999 by SMITHMARK Publishers,

a division of U.S. Media Holdings, Inc.,

115 West 18th Street, New York, NY 10011.

SMITHMARK books are available for bulk purchase for sales promotion and premium use. For details, write or call the manager of special sales, SMITHMARK Publishers, 115 West 18th Street, New York, NY 10011.

Creative Direction: Kristen Schilo, Gato & Maui Productions

Design: Galen Smith

ISBN: 0-7651-1057-1

Library of Congress Cataloging-in-Publication Data

Zebrowski, Carl.

Walking to Cold Mountain : a journey through Civil War America /
Carl Zebrowski : Foreword by Ken Burns.

    p.   cm.

Includes bibliographical references (p.   ) and index.

1. United States—History—Civil War, 1861-1865—Social aspects.

2. United States—History—Civil War, 1861-1865—Pictorial works.

3. United States—History—Civil War, 1861-1865—Miscellanea.

I. Title.

E468.9.Z43   1999

973.7—dc21   98-51960

                                                                   CIP

Printed in Hong Kong

10 9 8 7 6 5 4 3 2 1

~ DEDICATION ~

I must thank Robin, Chelsea, and Julian for their infinitely patient support. Robin
gracefully surveyed my work all along and offered valuable critiques. I couldn't have
finished my work without their help and understanding, and so I offer this book to
them as a token of appreciation.

PAGE TWO: A PRINCELY ABRAHAM LINCOLN REIGNS ALONGSIDE LIBERTY AND COLUMBIA
IN *THE OUTBREAK OF THE REBELLION OF THE UNITED STATES,* A POSTWAR PRINT CREATED
FOR SALE IN THE NORTH. PAGE SIX: ORGANIZED BY THE YOUNG MEN'S CHRISTIAN
ASSOCIATION IN 1861, THE UNITED STATES CHRISTIAN COMMISSION PROVIDED SOLDIERS
AT THE FRONT WITH NURSING CARE, COOKED FOOD, AND WRITING MATERIALS AND STAMPS.
ITS MAIN CHARGE, HOWEVER, WAS SPIRITUAL, AND ITS VOLUNTEERS DISTRIBUTED MILLIONS
OF BIBLES AND RELIGIOUS TRACTS.

CONTENTS

⸺ FOREWORD ⸺

In 1860, most of our nation's thirty-one million people lived peaceably on farms and in small towns. At Sharpsburg, Maryland, a German pacifist sect, the Dunkers, made their home in a sea of wheat and corn. At a small college in Gettysburg, Pennsylvania, population 2,400, young men studied Latin and mathematics. Steamboats filled with cotton came and went at Vicksburg high above the Mississippi. In Washington, D.C., Senator Jefferson Davis reviewed plans for re-modeling the Capitol. In Richmond, the 900 employees of the Tredegar Iron Works turned out gun carriages and cannon for the U.S. Government. At West Point, on the Hudson, officers trained, and friendships were formed they thought would last a lifetime. Within a few months everything would change.

At 4:30 A.M., on the fourteenth of April, in the year of our Lord Eighteen Hundred and Sixty-One, General Pierre Gustav Toutant Beauregard directed his Confederate gunners to open fire on Fort Sumter, at that hour only a dark shape out in the vastness of Charleston Harbor. The Civil War, our Civil War, had begun. Thirty-four hours later, a white flag over the fort ended the bombardment. The only casualty was a Confederate horse. It was a bloodless opening to the bloodiest war in American history, the most important struggle Americans have ever waged; a struggle, ultimately, for the very soul of the nation.

Surveying the cost of four seemingly endless years of unspeakable slaughter, the war's greatest chronicler, Shelby Foote, from the sad yet wise perspective of six score and three years, said simply that it was "the crossroads of our being." No one could have predicted the magnitude of the explosion that rocked America following that opening shot at Fort Sumter. Until then America had been, as historian Bruce Catton wrote, "small enough to carry in the mind and in the heart, and a young man's fatherland was what he could see from his bedroom window." Yet most of what America was before the Civil War went into sparking that explosion, and most of what the nation became resulted from it.

The steeple-less whitewashed church the Dunkers cherished found itself in the center of the battle of Antietam, where some of the bloodiest fighting in the bloodiest single day in our nation's history took place. The 2,400 inhabitants of Gettysburg soon found themselves tending to ten times that number of casualties during the greatest battle ever fought in the Western Hemisphere. Vicksburg's normally prosperous citizens were forced, during the Union siege, to live in caves, eat dog, and print their newspaper on the back of flowered wallpaper. In Washington, Lincoln insisted that work on the Capitol building go forward as a sign that the Union would survive, despite all matter of political intrigue in the city, enemy attacks that once nearly overran the capital, and covert action by numerous, usually ineffective, spies and one deadly assassin. Richmond was destroyed. And U.S. General Winfield Scott Hancock saw his close personal friend C.S.A. General Lewis A. Armistead killed by his own men during Pickett's Charge.

The Civil War has been given many names: the War Between the States, the War Against Northern Aggression, the Second American Revolution, the Lost Cause, the War of the Rebellion (that's the official name), the Brother's War, the Late Unpleasantness. Walt Whitman called it the War of Attempted Secession. Confederate General Joseph Johnston called it the War *Against* the States. By whatever name, it was unquestionably the most important event in the life of the nation.

It saw the end of slavery and the downfall of a southern planter's society. It was a watershed of a new political and economic order, and the beginning of big industry, big business, big government. It was the first truly modern war and, for Americans, the costliest, yielding the most American casualties and the greatest domestic suffering, spiritually and physically. It was the most horrible, necessary, intimate, acrimonious, mean-spirited, and heroic conflict the nation has known.

Inevitably, we grasp the war through such hyperbole. In so doing, we tend to blur the fact that real people lived through it and were changed by the event. One hundred eighty-five thousand black Americans fought to free their people. Fishermen and storekeepers from Deer Isle, Maine, served bravely and died miserably in strange places like Baton Rouge, Louisiana, and Fredericksburg, Virginia. There was scarcely a family in the South that did not lose a son or a brother or a father.

As with any civil strife, the war was marked by excruciating ironies. Robert E. Lee became a legend in the Confederate army only after turning down an offer to command the entire Union force. Four of Lincoln's own brothers-in-law fought on the Confederate side, and one was killed. The little town of Winchester, Virginia, changed hands seventy-two times during the war, and the state of Missouri sent thirty-nine regiments to fight in the siege of Vicksburg: seventeen to the Confederacy and twenty-two to the Union.

Few people have expressed these ironies, anomalies and divisions better than the poet Robert Penn Warren:

A civil war is, we may say, the prototype of all war, for in the persons of fellow citizens who happen to be the enemy we meet again with the old ambivalence of love and hate and with all the old guilts, the blood brothers of our childhood. In a civil war—especially one such as this when the nation shares deep and significant convictions and is not a mere handbasket of factions huddled arbitrarily together by historical happen-so—all the self-divisions of conflicts within individuals become a series of mirrors in which the plight of the country is reflected, and the self-division of the country a great mirror in which the individual may see imaged his own deep conflicts, not only the conflicts of political loyalties, but those more profoundly personal.

Our self-divisions were painfully reflected in the new medium of photography as well, which came of age during the Civil War. More than a million images were taken in four years for a public obsessed with seeing, and perhaps also thereby subduing, the shock and carnage they were inflicting on one another. It did not work. In late September, 1862, Mathew Brady opened an exhibition of war photographs entitled "The Dead of Antietam" at his New York City gallery. Nothing like them had ever been seen in America before. A reporter for the *New York Times* said it best:

The dead of the battle-field come up to us very rarely, even in dreams. We see the list [of dead and wounded] in the morning paper at breakfast, but dismiss its recollection with the coffee. There is a confused mass of names, but they are all strangers; we forget the horrible significance that dwells amid the jumble of type...We recognize the battle-field as a reality, but it stands as a remote one. It is like a funeral next door. It attracts your attention, but it does not enlist your sympathy. But it is very different when the hearse stops at your own door and the corpse is carried over your own threshold...Mr. Brady has done something to bring us the terrible reality and earnestness of the war. If he has not brought bodies and laid them in our door-yards and along [our] streets, he has done something very like it.

Ken Burns
Walpole, New Hampshire

My Dear Edward:—I have always been proud of you, and since your connection with the Confederate army, I have been prouder of you than ever before. I would not have you do anything wrong for the world, but before God, Edward, unless you come home, we must die. Last night, I was aroused by little Eddie's crying. I called and said 'What is the matter, Eddie?' and he said, 'O mamma! I am so hungry.' And Lucy, Edward, your darling Lucy; she never complains, but she is growing thinner and thinner every day. And before God, Edward, unless you come home, we must die.

Your Mary

Edward Cooper offered little defense at his court-martial hearing besides this personal letter from his distraught wife. Although it moved the court to tears, he was found guilty of deserting the Confederate army and sentenced to death. Only a late pardon from General Robert E. Lee spared his life.

By the end of the war, more than 300,000 soldiers, or about one out of every eight in the field, had fled from their armies. Bad food, shoddy clothing, problems with pay, boredom, lack of commitment, and the horrors of battle were just some of the things that drove them away. Many men, like Cooper, had loved ones at home who desperately needed help putting food on the table.

In Charles Frazier's novel *Cold Mountain*, the main character, Inman, a Confederate soldier from North Carolina, grows weary of the war's seemingly senseless slaughter and longs to be reunited with his sweetheart, Ada. Hospitalized with a neck wound in Raleigh, Inman slips away and heads west toward his home in the Blue Ridge Mountains.

This book was inspired by *Cold Mountain*, by Inman and the people he meets and the places he passes through while at war and on his way home, by Ada and folks like her facing daily trials on the home front. It's a figurative walk to Cold Mountain, a walk over battlegrounds and dirt roads, through towns and army camps, past farmers and slaves. It's a journey through early 1860s America, an America that was torn apart by civil war.

ABOVE: THIS ELEGANT VIRGINIA BELLE WEARS AN EXPENSIVE HAND-TAILORED DRESS AND FINE JEWELRY THAT SUGGEST A WEALTHY BACKGROUND. OPPOSITE: MORE TYPICAL OF WARTIME SOUTHERNERS WAS THIS NORTH CAROLINA PRIVATE ARMED WITH A FLINTLOCK MUSKET AND BOWIE KNIFE. HE WAS ONE OF ABOUT 125,000 TAR HEELS TO FIGHT IN THE CONFEDERATE ARMY.

To Arms!

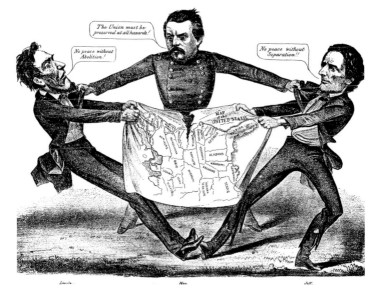

There was no turning back after Confederates bombarded Union-held Fort Sumter, South Carolina, on April 12, 1861. The tumultuous sectional conflict that extended back to America's Colonial days had finally come to war.

Patriotism swept through the North and South. Young women persuaded their sweethearts to join the army. Wives sent their husbands, and mothers sent their sons. Able-bodied men who stayed behind risked being ostracized by their families, friends, and neighbors.

War fever made it easy for Abraham Lincoln and Jefferson Davis to amass armies, at least at the start. On April 15, Lincoln called for 75,000 volunteers to bolster the 16,000-man prewar U.S. Army, and he soon had them. Southerners were just as quick to answer Davis's call for 82,000 men.

The citizen soldiers came from all walks of life. They were farmers and craftsmen, businessmen and politicians, fathers and sons. The more popular among them had the chance to be elected company officers. Others used political connections to obtain appointments. The rest became the rank and file.

At the heart of the widespread enthusiasm for sending men off to the armies was the prevailing belief that the war would be over in a matter of months. Accordingly, enlistment terms tended to be short, and the green troops marched off to the fields of battle confident that they would return home soon, bringing with them victory for their side.

OPPOSITE: THE U. S. CAPITOL BUILDING, LIKE THE AMERICAN EXPERIMENT IN DEMOCRACY IT SYMBOLIZED, WAS STILL A WORK-IN-PROGRESS ON MARCH 1, 1861, THE DAY OF ABRAHAM LINCOLN'S INAUGURATION. SEVEN SOUTHERN STATES HAD ALREADY SECEDED FROM THE UNION. ABOVE: UNION GENERAL GEORGE MCCLELLAN, REPRESENTING ADVOCATES OF COMPROMISE, TRIES TO KEEP LINCOLN AND JEFERSON DAVIS FROM TEARING THE COUNTRY IN TWO.

News of the attack on Fort Sumter and the flag at Charleston Harbor, South Carolina, was received in New York City late at night (13th April 1861) and was immediately sent out in extras of the newspapers....

Even after the bombardment of Sumter, however, the gravity of the revolt, and the power and will of the Slave States for a strong and continued military resistance to national authority were not at all realized at the North, except by a few. Nine tenths of the people of the Free States looked upon the rebellion as started in South Carolina from a feeling one half of contempt and the other half composed of anger and incredulity. It was not thought it would be joined by Virginia, North Carolina, or Georgia. A great cautious national official predicted that it would blow over "in sixty days," and folks generally believed the prediction.

WALT WHITMAN

BELOW: PROMINENT CITIZENS WERE CALLED UPON TO LEAD ARMY RECRUITMENT DRIVES IN THEIR HOME REGIONS. ONE METHOD THEY USED TO GET THE WORD OUT WAS POSTING PATRIOTIC SIGNS IN PUBLIC PLACES. RECRUITERS WHO SUCCESSFULLY RAISED REGIMENTS OFTEN WERE REWARDED WITH OFFICERS' COMMISSIONS.

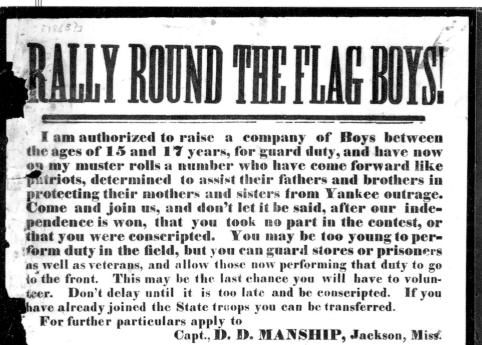

RALLY ROUND THE FLAG BOYS!

I am authorized to raise a company of Boys between the ages of 15 and 17 years, for guard duty, and have now on my muster rolls a number who have come forward like patriots, determined to assist their fathers and brothers in protecting their mothers and sisters from Yankee outrage. Come and join us, and don't let it be said, after our independence is won, that you took no part in the contest, or that you were conscripted. You may be too young to perform duty in the field, but you can guard stores or prisoners as well as veterans, and allow those now performing that duty to go to the front. This may be the last chance you will have to volunteer. Don't delay until it is too late and be conscripted. If you have already joined the State troops you can be transferred.
For further particulars apply to
Capt., D. D. MANSHIP, Jackson, Miss.

OPPOSITE: CONFEDERATE SERGEANT C. S. POWELL LOOKS YOUNGER THAN HE PROBABLY WAS, BUT IT WASN'T UNCOMMON FOR BOYS IN THEIR EARLY TEENS TO LIE ABOUT THEIR AGE SO THEY COULD FIGHT IN THE ARMIES. PRETEENS WHO REFUSED TO MISS THE ACTION JOINED REGIMENTAL BANDS, MOST FAMOUSLY AS DRUMMER BOYS.

All wars are boyish, and are fought by boys.

HERMAN MELVILLE

OPPOSITE: CONFEDERATE SOLDIER HAMILTON MCDEVIT BRANCH DRESSED IN HIS OGLETHORPE LIGHT INFANTRY UNIFORM FOR THIS KEEPSAKE PHOTO WITH JENNIE MCLAUGHLIN. ABOVE: WHEN THE TIME CAME TO PART, THERE WAS THE ALL-TOO-FAMILIAR GOOD-BYE SCENE, AN EMOTIONAL MOMENT THAT WOULD FASCINATE MANY AN ARTIST FOR YEARS TO COME.

You are going to the wars,

Willie boy, Willie boy,

You are going to the wars far away

To protect our rights and laws,

Willie boy, Willie boy,

And the banner in the sun's golden ray.

With your uniform so new,

And your shining buttons too,

You'll win the hearts of pretty girls,

But none like me so true.

Oh, won't you think of me,

Willie boy, Willie boy?

Oh, won't you think of me when far away?

I'll often think of ye,

Willie boy, Willie boy,

And ever for your life and glory pray.

FROM THE SONG

"YOU ARE GOING TO THE WARS,

WILLIE BOY!"

FROM REVEILLE TO TAPS

packed up his gear for a march over muddy roads, or fell into formation with his unit for drills intended to turn him into a disciplined, efficient soldier. For dinner, he could look forward to fresh beef, warm bread, a baked potato, a spoonful of peas, and a cup of coffee during the best of times. Salt pork and hardtack (a rock-hard biscuit made of flour and water) were better than nothing at all. The weary troop's day ended with another bugle call.

y July 1861, a few hundred thousand soldiers were dressed in blue and gray and eager for the glory of battle. But instead of getting the chance to become heroes, they got to sit in camp and wait. Even as the war heated up, the average fighting man still spent most of his time doing something other than fighting.

The soldier's life was one of tedious chores, bland food, leaky tents, exhausting marches, and monotonous drills. In the morning, a private might have awakened to an insistent bugle call and crawled out of a tent soaking wet from an overnight rain. Perhaps he ate a modest breakfast and then scrubbed his laundry in a metal basin,

OPPOSITE: MEMBERS OF THE 9TH MISSISSIPPI'S COMPANY B AWAIT A MEAL IN A TYPICAL RUSTIC ARMY CAMP. KINLOCK FALCONER, A FUTURE MEMBER OF CONFEDERATE GENERAL BRAXTON BRAGG'S STAFF, FRIES PORK OVER HOT COALS. **LEFT:** A CONFEDERATE SOLDIER POSES FOR A *CARTE-DE-VISITE* IMAGE IN PRISTINE SURROUNDINGS THAT WERE FAR DIFFERENT FROM THOSE HE WOULD FIND IN CAMP. BEFORE LEAVING HOME, SOLDIERS OFTEN GAVE FRIENDS AND LOVED ONES PERSONAL MEMENTOS SUCH AS *CARTES DE VISITE,* HEAVY-PAPER CALLING CARDS WITH PHOTOGRAPHS PRINTED ON THEM.

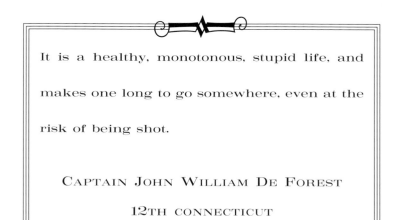

It is a healthy, monotonous, stupid life, and makes one long to go somewhere, even at the risk of being shot.

CAPTAIN JOHN WILLIAM DE FOREST
12TH CONNECTICUT

WHEN I GET HOME I SHALL BE qualified for any position, either that of boot black, a cleaner of brasses, a washer-(wo)man, cook, chambermaid, hewer of wood and drawer of water, or, failing in all these I can turn beggar and go from door to door asking for "broken vittles." In all these I should feel perfectly at home by long practise therein.

SAMUEL STORROW

MASSACHUSETTS VOLUNTEER

BELOW: IN CAMP, SOLDIERS HAD TO TAKE CARE OF DUTIES THAT PERHAPS THEIR WIVES USUALLY ASSUMED AT HOME. ONE WAS WASHING LAUNDRY, A TASK PRECEDED BY THE HAULING OF SEVERAL GALLONS OF WATER TO FILL A LARGE WASH BASIN.
OPPOSITE: IT WAS ALREADY AN ARMY TRADITION FOR TROOPS TO COMPLAIN ABOUT THEIR FOOD. THE COOKS NO DOUBT APPRECIATED NEITHER THE CHORE OF PREPARING THE MEALS NOR THEIR COMRADES' DERISIVE REMARKS.

LEFT: THE PERENNIAL FAVORITE BEVERAGE OF THE BORED AND THE BURDENED, ALCOHOL WAS A PRIZED COMMODITY IN CAMP. THESE WELL-PREPARED TROOPS HAD THEIR OWN MAKESHIFT WINE CELLAR HIDDEN BENEATH A WOODEN FLOOR. BELOW: AS DIVERSIONS GO, MUSIC WAS LESS EXPENSIVE AND MORE WIDELY AVAILABLE THAN ALCOHOL. HERE, A FIDDLER PLAYS AN INSTRUMENT FASHIONED FROM A CIGAR BOX TO PASS TIME IN CAMP.

We're tenting tonight on the old Camp
ground,

Give us a song to cheer

Our weary hearts, a song of home,

And Friends we love so dear.

Many are the hearts that are weary

tonight,

Wishing for the war to cease,

Many are the hearts looking for the

right

To see the dawn of peace.

Tenting tonight, Tenting tonight,

Tenting on the old Camp ground.

FROM THE SONG

"TENTING ON THE OLD CAMP GROUND"

LEFT: IN THE DAYS BEFORE AUDIO RECORDING, THE MUSIC
BUSINESS, SUCH AS IT WAS, MADE ITS MONEY THROUGH THE
SALE OF SHEET MUSIC. THE REBEL SONG "DIXIE'S LAND," OR
SIMPLY "DIXIE," WAS SO POPULAR BACK HOME AND IN CAMP
THAT ONE ENTERPRISING PUBLISHER RELEASED A VERSION OF IT
WITH REVISED WORDS FOR NORTHERNERS (TOP LEFT).

WHAT PRICE GLORY?

OPPOSITE: AS CIVIL WAR BATTLES BECAME MORE DEADLY, SOLDIERS HAD MORE TO WORRY ABOUT THAN EVERYDAY TEDIUM. A LITHOGRAPH ENTITLED *THE AMERICAN PATRIOT'S DREAM* DEPICTS A SOLDIER'S ANXIOUS PREOCCUPATIONS ON THE NIGHT BEFORE A BATTLE. **BELOW:** SERIOUS FIGHTING BROUGHT SERIOUS WEAPONRY. THE LEMAT PISTOL, WHICH INMAN CARRIED, WAS A NINE-SHOT .40-CALIBER REVOLVER EQUIPPED WITH A SECOND BARREL THAT FIRED A LOAD LIKE A SAWED-OFF SHOTGUN.

After a year of relatively minor battles that created a false sense of security in the North and South, Confederate and Union armies met at Pittsburg Landing, Tennessee, on April 6 and 7, 1862. Here, near a small meetinghouse called Shiloh Church, 110,000 men fought in the war's first great bloody clash. The Battle of Shiloh ended with 24,000 men killed, wounded, or captured.

Before year's end, there were more costly battles, notably the Battle of Antietam, fought at Sharpsburg, Maryland, on September 17. By nightfall there were 26,000 casualties, making it the bloodiest day in the whole war. Bodies of Confederate troops lay piled in the Sunken Road, a small dirt byway that passed into history with the name Bloody Lane.

The horror of these battles convinced even stubborn optimists that this war was real. So it would remain for three more years.

> We shall be in one of the bloodiest wars that history has recorded.
>
> ALEXANDER STEPHENS
> VICE PRESIDENT OF THE CONFEDERACY

> ## D
> EATH IS NOTHING HERE. AS YOU step out in the morning from your tent to wash your face, you see before you on a stretcher a shapeless, extended object, and over it is thrown a dark gray blanket. It is the corpse of some wounded or sick soldier of the regiment who died in the hospital tent during the night; perhaps there is a row of three or four of these corpses lying covered over. No one makes an ado.
>
> WALT WHITMAN

RIGHT: ALL SORTS OF BUILDINGS WERE TURNED INTO HOSPITALS TO ACCOMMODATE THE GROWING NUMBERS OF WOUNDED SOLDIERS. THIS PUBLIC BUILDING IN WASHINGTON'S ARMORY SQUARE WAS FAR MORE SPACIOUS AND COMFORTABLE THAN MOST TEMPORARY MEDICAL FACILITIES. INSET: DOCTORS DIDN'T YET KNOW MUCH ABOUT PREVENTING INFECTION AND CONTROLLING THE SPREAD OF DISEASE, SO MANY SOLDIERS TAKEN TO ARMY HOSPITALS DIED THERE. AMBITIOUS MORTICIANS DIDN'T MISS THE OPPORTUNITY TO TURN THE TRAGEDY INTO PROFIT.

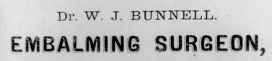

Dr. W. J. BUNNELL.

EMBALMING SURGEON,

Has been with the Army

Since its advance to White House, Harrison's Landing, Sharpsburg, Antietam, Fredericksburg, Chancellorsville, and Gettysburg, during which time he has embalmed a large number of bodies with Dr. Holmes' process, invariably giving the best satisfaction.

Office, Branty Station, Va.

OPPOSITE: BODIES OF CONFEDERATE SOLDIERS FILL BLOODY LANE AFTER THE SEPTEMBER 17, 1862, BATTLE OF ANTIETAM IN SHARPSBURG, MARYLAND. RIGHT: BY THE END OF DECEMBER 13, THE SCENE AT FREDERICKSBURG, VIRGINIA, WAS SIMILAR TO BLOODY LANE, EXCEPT HERE THE DEAD WERE UNION MEN PILED BEFORE THE INFAMOUS STONE WALL AT THE FOOT OF MARYE'S HEIGHTS. BELOW: REPRESENTING AN INCREDULOUS NORTHERN CITIZENRY, COLUMBIA DEMANDS THAT LINCOLN EXPLAIN THE FREDERICKSBURG DISASTER.

> It is well that war is so terrible, or we should grow too fond of it.
>
> ROBERT E. LEE
> DURING THE BATTLE OF FREDERICKSBURG

COLUMBIA. "Where are my 15,000 Sons—murdered at Fredericksburg?"   LINCOLN. "This reminds me of a little Joke—"   COLUMBIA. "Go tell your Joke AT SPRINGFIELD!!"

EYES *OF* THE NATIONS

ever before did so many people back home learn so much about a war as quickly as they did during the Civil War. Correspondents following the armies delivered reports to newspapers, which printed them in daily and weekly editions. Illustrated papers such as *Harper's Weekly* and *Frank Leslie's Illustrated Newspaper* in New York City had staff artists in the field who sent back sketches that were turned into engravings for publication. Together, the written accounts and artistic interpretations of battles and army life gave civilians an unprecedented look at the workings of war.

Similarly, war had never been so thoroughly documented in photographs. Recent technological advancements enabled photographers to travel with extensive camera equipment and portable darkrooms. Working in the field, they exposed scenes onto photographic plates that were then developed in darkrooms. Prints were made from the negative plates in large quantities and sold. The profits funded the world's first great photographic history of a nation at war.

ABOVE: ALFRED R. WAUD OF *HARPER'S WEEKLY* WAS THE MOST PROLIFIC OF ALL BATTLEFIELD ARTISTS WORKING FOR ILLUSTRATED NEWSPAPERS. **INSET:** AT APPOMATTOX COURT HOUSE, WAUD CAPTURED A SOLEMN GENERAL ROBERT E. LEE LEAVING THE MCLEAN HOUSE AFTER SURRENDERING HIS ARMY ON APRIL 9, 1865, EFFECTIVELY ENDING THE WAR. **OPPOSITE:** A BILLBOARD AT THE *PITTSBURGH DISPATCH* OFFICE TEASES POTENTIAL NEWSPAPER BUYERS ON JUNE 9, 1862, WITH THE LINES "LATER FROM RICHMOND AND MEMPHIS, GEN. MCCLELLAN'S REPORT OF THE BATTLE, OUR LOSS IN KILLED AND WOUNDED AND MISSING 5,134." **OPPOSITE INSETS:** THE FLAMBOYANT A. P. MUBEN AND OTHER NEWSPAPER VENDORS HAWKED PUBLICATIONS SUCH AS THE *SUNDAY MAGAZINE*.

BELOW: NORTHERN FIELD PHOTOGRAPHERS CELEBRATE THE END OF THE WAR AT MANASSAS, VIRGINIA, THE SITE OF THE WAR'S FIRST BATTLE—THE JULY 21, 1861, BATTLE OF BULL RUN. THE MOST FAMOUS AMONG THEM, ALEXANDER GARDNER, IS SEATED AT THE FAR LEFT. BELOW RIGHT: FOR FOUR YEARS, CAMERAMEN PLIED THEIR TRADE IN THE FIELD, CAPTURING WAR SCENES FOR THE MASSES WHILE PROVIDING IMPORTANT SERVICES TO THE UNION ARMIES. HERE, A MAP IS BEING PHOTOGRAPHED SO IT CAN BE REPRODUCED AND DISTRIBUTED TO COMMANDERS. OPPOSITE: PHOTOGRAPHERS TRAVELED WITH GENERAL GEORGE B. MCCLELLAN'S ARMY DURING THE 1862 PENINSULA CAMPAIGN, DOCUMENTING THE UNION'S FAILED THREE-MONTH DRIVE UP THE VIRGINIA PENINSULA TO CAPTURE THE CONFEDERATE CAPITAL. OPPOSITE INSET: PHOTOGRAPHERS ENDURED MANY OF THE SAME HARDSHIPS THE SOLDIERS DID, INCLUDING BRAVING THE EAST COAST'S BRISK WINTERS IN CRUDE LOG HUTS.

Photography was never before applied to so important an object, and it rarely, if ever, produced such brilliant and satisfactory results.

FROM A POSTWAR CATALOGUE OF
MATHEW BRADY'S WAR PHOTOS

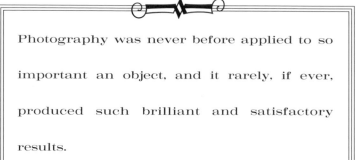

I felt I had to go. A spirit in my feet said

"go" and I went.

MATHEW BRADY

FAILING IN EYESIGHT, MATHEW BRADY (LEFT) SENT EMPLOYEES TO FOL-LOW THE ARMIES WHILE HE REMAINED MOSTLY IN HIS STUDIO. HIS CREWS TOOK THOUSANDS OF PHOTOS, WHICH HE STAMPED WITH HIS OWN IMPRINT. THUS, HE MADE HIM-SELF THE MOST FAMOUS OF ALL CIVIL WAR PHOTOGRAPHERS, POSSIBLY WITHOUT TAKING A SINGLE SHOT IN THE FIELD. HE DID, HOWEVER, PHOTOGRAPH MANY OF THE WAR'S HEROES, INCLUD-ING GENERALS ROBERT E. LEE (FAR LEFT) AND ULYSSES S. GRANT (TOP). **OPPOSITE**: WORKERS IN AN ENGLISH SHOP MASS-PRODUCE PRINTS TO SELL TO A PUBLIC ENTHRALLED BY THE NEW PHOTOGRAPHIC TECHNOLOGY AND ITS POSSIBILITIES. IN AMERICA, DURING THE 1860S, PEOPLE WERE EAGERLY SPENDING THEIR MONEY ON WAR PHOTOS.

HEARTLAND OF THE SOUTH

This was true in both the North and South, but it is the rural *South* that stirs the imagination. Movies, television shows, and novels have portrayed it as a tranquil world of drooping trees, pastel magnolia blossoms, and gentle creeks, of well-bred gentlemen and soft-spoken ladies, sturdy common folks, and noble slaves. Surely some of this idealistic image owed to artistic license, but the inspiration for it was real enough.

Though cities and factories had begun to take over the countryside, mid-nineteenth-century America was still a land of rivers and streams, mountains and hills, fields and plains. The average American lived in a rural area.

THE WINDINGS OF THE MIGHTY river, the endless cypress forests in the background, the vast fields of cane and corn, the abundant magnolias and orange groves and bananas, the plantation houses showing white through dark-green foliage furnished an uninterrupted succession of lovely pictures.

CAPTAIN JOHN WILLIAM DE FOREST
12TH CONNECTICUT

BELOW: A few rural folks gather at a cottage at Virginia's Cedar Mountain. Though neighbors sometimes lived far apart, they visited one another for companionship and to help with chores. **LEFT:** Rare was the backcountryman without a musket. He used it to hunt game, protect his crops from destructive varmints, and scare away unwelcome visitors. A dog was helpful, too.

Oh, yes, I am a Southern girl,

And glory in the name,

And boast it with far greater pride

Than glittering wealth or fame.

We envy not the Northern girl,

Her robes of beauty rare,

Though diamonds grace her snowy neck,

And pearls bedeck her hair.

FROM THE SONG

"THE HOMESPUN DRESS"

RIGHT: THE COMMON ATTIRE FOR A RURAL WOMAN WAS A SIMPLE LONG DRESS OR A LONG SKIRT AND BLOUSE. SHE OWNED FEW OUTFITS AND PROBABLY SEWED THEM HERSELF. SHE ALSO MADE CLOTHES FOR THE REST OF HER FAMILY.

We were told so frequently—"My father was killed in those woods" or "The guerrillas shot my brother in that ravine"....

ALBERT D. RICHARDSON

NEW YORK TRIBUNE CORRESPONDENT

IN THE NORTH CAROLINA MOUNTAINS

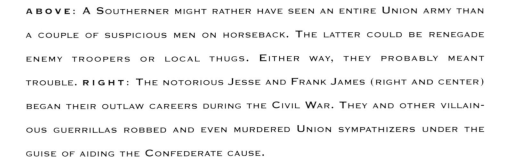

ABOVE: A SOUTHERNER MIGHT RATHER HAVE SEEN AN ENTIRE UNION ARMY THAN A COUPLE OF SUSPICIOUS MEN ON HORSEBACK. THE LATTER COULD BE RENEGADE ENEMY TROOPERS OR LOCAL THUGS. EITHER WAY, THEY PROBABLY MEANT TROUBLE. RIGHT: THE NOTORIOUS JESSE AND FRANK JAMES (RIGHT AND CENTER) BEGAN THEIR OUTLAW CAREERS DURING THE CIVIL WAR. THEY AND OTHER VILLAINOUS GUERRILLAS ROBBED AND EVEN MURDERED UNION SYMPATHIZERS UNDER THE GUISE OF AIDING THE CONFEDERATE CAUSE.

RIGHT: CHORES FILLED THE HOMEMAKER'S DAY. BUTTER HAD TO BE CHURNED. CLOTHES HAD TO BE SCRUBBED AGAINST A WASHBOARD. DINNER HAD TO BE MADE FROM SCRATCH.
BELOW: FARMS AND CROPS HAD TO BE TENDED, TOO, BY MEN, WOMEN, CHILDREN, WHOMEVER WAS AVAILABLE. MORE OFTEN THAN NOT, FARM WORK INCLUDED MAINTAINING A CORN FIELD, SUCH AS THIS ONE NEAR ANNAPOLIS, MARYLAND.

I have never rebelled at hard, clean work, like haying or harvest, but the slavery of being nurse to calves and scrub-boy to horses cankered my spirits.

ANONYMOUS FARM WORKER

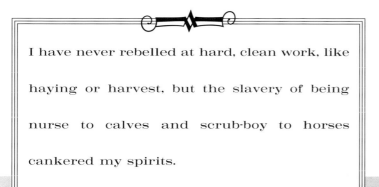

LEFT: WHAT THE BACK-COUNTRY DWELLER COULDN'T SUPPLY FOR HIMSELF, HE FOUND IN TOWN. GENERAL STORES SOLD MEATS, FRUITS AND VEGETABLES, BOOKS AND STATIONERY, AND OTHER NECESSITIES. COOLEY'S, IN THE COASTAL TOWN OF BEAUFORT, SOUTH CAROLINA, EVEN SOLD PHOTOGRAPHS, IMAGES SHOT BY STORE PROPRIETOR SAMUEL A. COOLEY (LEANING ON THE WAGON). ABOVE: ONE OF HUNDREDS OF COOLEY PHOTOS DOCUMENTING WARTIME SOUTH CAROLINA, THIS VIEW SHOWS BAY STREET IN BEAUFORT, A TYPICAL SOUTHERN TOWN.

The rule in North Carolina seems to be that it takes two houses to make a town and that three and a barn constitute a city.

SAMUEL STORROW
MASSACHUSETTS VOLUNTEER

THE CITIES

C ities grew faster than ever from the dawn of the nineteenth century to the start of the Civil War. By 1860, twelve percent of the American population lived in cities with more than 25,000 people, where there were unprecedented economic, cultural, and educational opportunities. New York, home to a million people and a thriving business community, was already one of the largest cities in the world. Philadelphia had half a million people, and Boston 200,000.

Southern cities were much smaller, but they were big enough to attract the attention of Union armies. New Orleans, with a population of 100,000, was one of the first targets, and on April 25, 1862, it fell into enemy hands. Over the next three years, many more Southern cities followed.

RIGHT: PORT CITIES SUCH AS ADA'S NATIVE CHARLESTON, SOUTH CAROLINA, THRIVED OFF THE IMPORT AND EXPORT BUSINESS UNTIL THE UNION BLOCKADE OF THE SOUTHERN COASTS HALTED SHIPPING TRAFFIC. OPPOSITE: INLAND CITIES DEPENDED ON TRAINS TO BRING IN AND SEND OUT GOODS. ATLANTA, A MAJOR RAILROAD HUB, HAD BUSTLING STREETS BEFORE THE WAR.

HARPER'S
NEW MONTHLY MAGAZINE.
No. LXXXV.—JUNE, 1857.—Vol. XV.

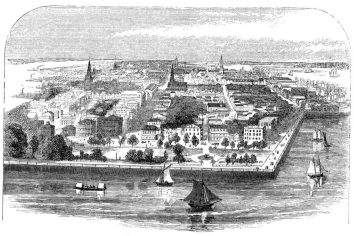

BIRD'S-EYE VIEW OF THE PALMETTO CITY.

THE POVERTY OF THE ONCE flourishing city of New Orleans is astonishing. I have seen nothing like its desolation since I quitted the deserted streets of Venice, Ferrara and Pisa. Almost the only people visible are shabby roughs and ragged beggars. Many poor Irish and Germans hang about our regiments begging for the refuse of our rations. The town is fairly and squarely on the point of starvation. No one denies now that our blockade has been effective; it kept out everything, even to the yellow fever.

JOHN WILLIAM DE FOREST
12TH CONNECTICUT

OPPOSITE TOP: BY WAR'S END, CONFEDERATE MONEY WAS ALL BUT WORTHLESS. EVEN IN THE SOUTH, UNITED STATES CURRENCY WAS THE PREFERRED PAYMENT. OPPOSITE BOTTOM: ON THE TENNESSEE RIVER, THE *CHICKAMAUGA* DELIVERS A LOAD OF SALT PORK TO UNION TROOPS IN CHATTANOOGA IN 1863. BY THIS TIME, THE UNION CONTROLLED THE SOUTH'S MAJOR RIVERS, SO SOUTHERN VESSELS COULD NOT SAFELY NAVIGATE THEM. TOP RIGHT: THE ANTEBELLUM DAYS BROUGHT ALL SORTS OF CIVILIAN TRAVELERS TO HOTELS ALONG THE MISSISSIPPI RIVER. THE WAR BROUGHT UNION SOLDIERS INSTEAD. BOTTOM RIGHT: TROOPS IN BLUE EVENTUALLY BROKE THROUGH TO CHARLESTON, AND ON FEBRUARY 17, 1865, CITIZENS WERE FORCED TO EVACUATE.

WHAT A CONTRAST DID THE GAY, wealthy city of New York afford at this period to my own sorrow-stricken land! Here there was no sign of want or poverty. No woebegone faces could I see in that assemblage: all was life and animation. Though war raged within a short distance, its horrors had little influence on the butterflies of the Empire City; whilst in my own dear native country, all was sad and heart-rending. We were sacrificing lives upon the altar of Liberty; while the North sacrificed hers upon the altar of Mammon.

BELLE BOYD

CONFEDERATE SPY

TOP RIGHT: UNLIKE IN MANY ENEMY-OCCUPIED SOUTHERN CITIES, DAILY LIFE PROCEEDED MORE OR LESS NORMALLY HERE AT CITY HALL AND ELSEWHERE IN NEW YORK CITY. BOTTOM RIGHT: THE LATEST FASHIONS WERE STILL AVAILABLE TO THOSE WHO COULD AFFORD THEM. OPPOSITE: A STREET VENDOR SELLS SARSAPARILLA AND BEER AT THREE CENTS A GLASS IN THIS VIEW LOOKING EAST ON A LIVELY BROADWAY.

Fashions for September.

...ished by Mr. G. BRODIE, 300 *Canal Street, New York, and drawn by* VOIGT *from actual articles of Costume.*

FIGURES 1 AND 2.—DINNER TOILET AND PROMENADE COSTUME.

LIBERTY *AND* JUSTICE *FOR ALL*

s slaveholding in America approached its 250th year, the country's slave population reached four million in 1860. A quarter of all Southern families owned slaves. Ten thousand of them owned fifty or more, while the average slaveholder owned ten to twenty.

Slaves spent their days toiling in tobacco, rice, sugar, and cotton fields, tending small farms, or working as craftsmen and domestic servants. If they didn't live up to their masters' standards, they faced whipping or some other harsh penalty.

Slaves were finally given hope for a better future when Lincoln delivered his Emancipation Proclamation, which took effect on January 1, 1863. Though slaveholders had no intention of heeding the enemy president's order to free all slaves in the rebellious states, it was clear the war had evolved from a fight to preserve the Union to a fight to end slavery forever.

Sale of Slaves and Stock.

The Negroes and Stock listed below, are a Prime Lot, and belong to the ESTATE OF THE LATE LUTHER McGOWAN, and will be sold on Monday, Sept. 22nd, 1852, at the Fair Grounds, in Savannah, Georgia, at 1:00 P. M. The Negroes will be taken to the grounds two days previous to the Sale, so that they may be inspected by prospective buyers.

On account of the low prices listed below, they will be sold for cash only, and must be taken into custody within two hours after sale.

No.	Name.	Age.	Remarks.	Price.
1	Lunesta	27	Prime Rice Planter,	$1,275.00
2	Violet	16	Housework and Nursemaid,	900.00
3	Lizzie	30	Rice, Unsound,	300.00
4	Minda	27	Cotton, Prime Woman,	1,200.00
5	Adam	28	Cotton, Prime Young Man,	1,100.00
6	Abel	41	Rice Hand, Eyesight Poor,	675.00
7	Tanney	22	Prime Cotton Hand,	950.00
8	Flementina	39	Good Cook. Stiff Knee,	400.00
9	Lanney	34	Prime Cottom Man,	1,000.00
10	Sally	10	Handy in Kitchen,	675.00
11	Maccabey	35	Prime Man, Fair Carpenter,	980.00
12	Dorcas Judy	25	Seamstress, Handy in House,	800.00
13	Happy	60	Blacksmith,	575.00
14	Mowden	15	Prime Cotton Boy,	700.00
15	Bills	21	Handy with Mules,	900.00
16	Theopolis	39	Rice Hand, Gets Fits,	575.00
17	Coolidge	29	Rice Hand and Blacksmith,	1,275.00
18	Bessie	69	Infirm, Sews,	250.00
19	Infant	1	Strong Likely Boy,	400.00
20	Samson	41	Prime Man, Good with Stock,	975.00
21	Callie May	27	Prime Woman, Rice,	1,000.00
22	Honey	14	Prime Girl, Hearing Poor,	850.00
23	Angelina	16	Prime Girl, House or Field,	1,000.00
24	Virgil	21	Prime Field Hand,	1,100.00
25	Tom	40	Rice Hand, Lame Leg,	750.00
26	Noble	11	Handy Boy,	900.00
27	Judge Lesh	55	Prime Blacksmith,	800.00
28	Booster	43	Fair Mason, Unsound,	600.00
29	Big Kate	37	Housekeeper and Nurse,	950.00
30	Melie Ann	19	Housework, Smart Yellow Girl,	1,250.00
31	Deacon	26	Prime Rice Hand,	1,000.00
32	Coming	19	Prime Cotton Hand,	1,000.00
33	Mabel	47	Prime Cotton Hand,	800.00
34	Uncle Tim	60	Fair Hand with Mules,	600.00
35	Abe	27	Prime Cotton Hand,	1,000.00
36	Tennes	29	Prime Rice Hand and Coachman,	1,250.00

There will also be offered at this sale, twenty head of Horses and Mules with harness, along with thirty head of Prime Cattle. Slaves will be sold separate, or in lots, as best suits the purchaser. Sale will be held rain or shine.

ABOVE: SLAVES WERE TREATED LIKE ANY OTHER PROPERTY. WHEN AN OWNER DIED, HIS SLAVES WERE LEFT TO HEIRS OR SOLD OFF. RIGHT: COTTON-FIELD WORKERS CARRY IN THEIR HARVEST IN A POSTWAR PHOTO OF A PLANTATION NEAR CHARLESTON. THOUGH MACHINES PROCESSED THE COTTON, THE TEDIOUS PICKING STILL HAD TO BE DONE BY HAND.

I never knew a man who wished himself to be a slave. Consider if you know any good thing that no man desires for himself.

ABRAHAM LINCOLN

Genealogical trees do not flourish among slaves. A person of some consequence here in the north, sometimes designated father, is literally abolished in slave law and slave practice.

FREDERICK DOUGLASS

OPPOSITE: A FAMILY OF SLAVES POSES IN FRONT OF ITS QUARTERS ON A SOUTH CAROLINA COTTON PLANTATION. FEW FAMILIES IN BONDAGE WERE FORTUNATE ENOUGH TO REMAIN INTACT, AS SLAVEHOLDERS ROUTINELY BROKE THEM UP. **ABOVE:** SOME SLAVES BECAME MORE OR LESS PART OF THEIR MASTER'S FAMILIES. HERE IS A RARE PHOTO OF A SLAVE NANNY AND ONE OF HER MASTER'S CHILDREN ENTRUSTED TO HER CARE. **LEFT:** SLAVES PLANT THE FIELDS ON POPE'S PLANTATION AT HILTON HEAD, SOUTH CAROLINA. THE REWARDS FOR THEIR LABOR WERE LITTLE MORE THAN SHELTER IN A CRUDE SHACK AND A DAILY RATION OF ONE OR TWO POUNDS OF CORN AND A HALF-POUND OF SALT PORK.

You have seen how a man was made a slave; you shall see how a slave was made a man.

FREDERICK DOUGLASS

OPPOSITE: A UNION CORPORAL STANDS WITH A RIFLE AND FIXED BAYONET. MORE THAN 180,000 BLACK MEN FOUGHT IN THE UNION MILITARY. ABOVE: THOUGH MOST OF THEM SERVED WITH THE ARMY, SOME WERE WITH THE NAVY. THESE FORMER SLAVES POSE ABOARD THE U.S.S. VERMONT OFF HILTON HEAD, SOUTH CAROLINA, IN 1863. RIGHT: AFTER THE WAR, THOUSANDS OF FREED SLAVES SUDDENLY FOUND THEMSELVES ON THEIR OWN. TEACHERS FROM THE NORTH, KNOWN AS GIDEONITES, TRAVELED SOUTH TO HELP PREPARE THEM FOR THEIR NEW LIVES.

THE BITTERSWEET END

THE BEAUTIFUL HOMESTEADS OF the parish country, with their wonderful tropical gardens, were ruined, ancient dwellings of black cypress, one hundred years old, which had been reared by the fathers of the republic—men whose names were famous in Revolutionary history—were given to the torch as recklessly as were the rude hovels; choice pictures and works of art, from Europe, select and numerous libraries, objects of peace wholly, were all destroyed.

WILLIAM GILMORE SIMMS

SOUTHERN WRITER

ON THE DESTRUCTION

OF COLUMBIA, SOUTH CAROLINA

A lmost four years to the day after the war had begun at Fort Sumter, General Robert E. Lee surrendered his army to General Ulysses S. Grant at Appomattox Court House, Virginia. It was April 9, 1865, and with the South's greatest army giving up the fight, the four darkest years in American history had come to an end.

But the tragedy didn't suddenly disappear. There was the painful realization that 625,000 Americans had died, as many as would die in all other American wars combined. Then Lincoln was assassinated on the night of April 14, as he watched the play *Our American Cousin* at Ford's Theatre in Washington, D.C. In retaliation, Jefferson Davis was arrested on May 10 in Irwinsville, Georgia, and imprisoned for two years.

Eventually the country moved on. Soldiers who survived the fighting returned to their families. Whatever the North and South won and lost in the war, the slaves were finally free, and the future was sure to be better than the past four years had been.

OPPOSITE: GENERAL JOHN MCCAUSLAND'S CONFEDERATES DESTROYED TWO-THIRDS OF CHAMBERSBURG, PENNSYLVANIA, ON JULY 30 AND 31, 1864. DAMAGES REACHED ALMOST $1.5 MILLION. MOST OF THE PROPERTY DESTROYED DURING THE WAR, HOWEVER, STOOD ON SOUTHERN GROUND.

ABOVE: SOME 625,000 SOLDIERS PAID THE ULTIMATE PRICE FOR THEIR CAUSE. AS REMINDERS OF THEIR SACRIFICE, ROWS AND ROWS OF GRAVE MARKERS FILL MILITARY CEMETERIES SUCH AS THIS ONE AT ALEXANDRIA, VIRGINIA. OPPOSITE: EVEN ABRAHAM LINCOLN BECAME A MARTYR FOR HIS CAUSE. THIS IMAGE, THE ONLY KNOWN POSTMORTEM PHOTO OF HIM, WAS TAKEN AT NEW YORK CITY HALL. SECRETARY OF STATE EDWIN STANTON THOUGHT IT WAS IN POOR TASTE AND ORDERED THE NEGATIVE DESTROYED, BUT ONE PRINT SURVIVED.

I could not help thinking how ridiculous our world must appear to superior intelligences—our incurring so much trouble, expense and suffering to maim and murder each other....

ANN R. L. SCHAEFFER
VISITOR AT A UNION HOSPITAL

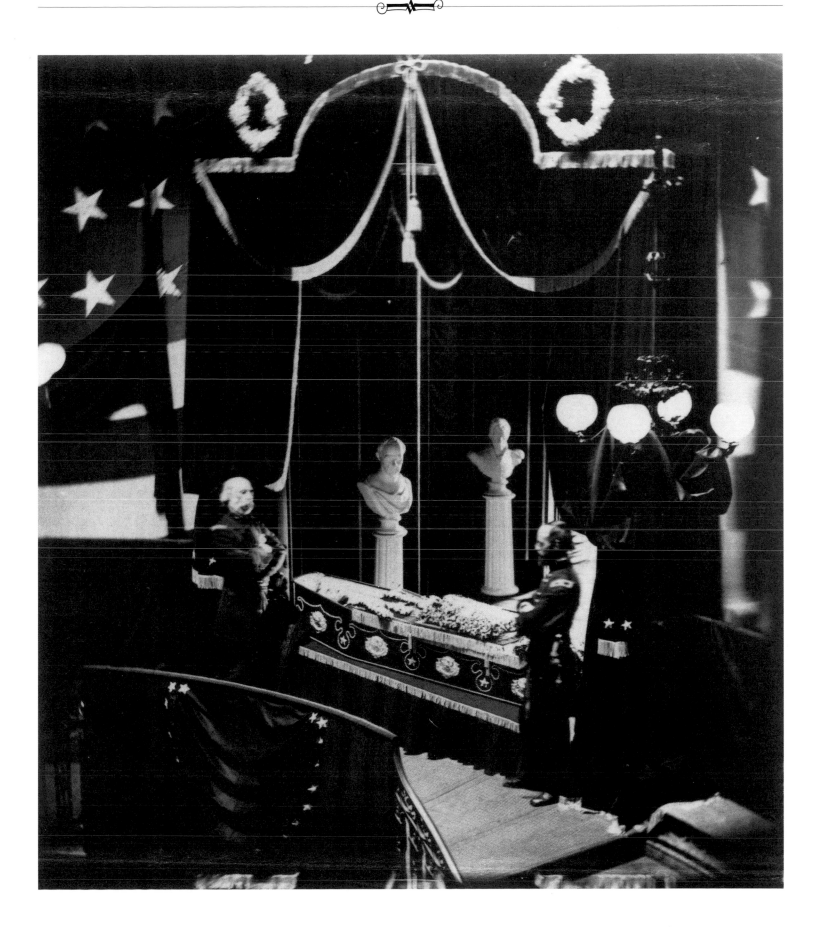

All the privation and starvation and blood-stains of the past four years, and the woes and trials, griefs and fears, of those last dreadful days were swept away by those blessed, precious words, "Whoa, Lucy!" spoken in my husband's tender tones.

LaSalle "Lucy" Corbell Pickett
on the return of her husband,
George, from the war

RIGHT: A Union prisoner of war is reunited with his sweetheart after returning home from Georgia's infamous Andersonville Prison. Though too many soldiers had died in four years, including more than 13,000 at Andersonville, a majority of them eventually made it back home to their families. Inman finally reached his destination of Cold Mountain for an ecstatic, yet heart-rending, reunion with his beloved Ada.

~ ILLUSTRATION CREDITS ~

Page 2: Library of Congress; **Page 6:** Library of Congress; **Page 10:** James C. Frasca; **Page 11:** Herb Peck, Jr.; **Page 12:** Library of Congress; **Pages 13 and 14:** *Civil War Times;* **Page 15:** Bentonville Battleground State Historic Site; **Page 16:** Herb Peck, Jr.; **Page 17:** Library of Congress; **Page 18:** *Civil War Times;* **Page 19:** Library of Congress; **Page 20:** United States Army Military History Institute; **Page 21:** National Archives; **Page 22:** United States Army Military History Institute (top), Library of Congress (bottom); **Page 23:** *Civil War Times;* **Page 24:** Library of Congress; **Page 25:** United States Army; **Page 26:** National Archives; **Page 27:** *Civil War Times* (inset); **Page 28:** United States Army Military History Institute (top), *Civil War Times* (bottom); **Page 29:** United States Army Military History Institute; **Page 30:** Library of Congress (both); **Page 31:** Mrs. Albert McBride, *Civil War Times* (top inset), Library of Congress (bottom inset); **Page 32:** Library of Congress (inset), Larry J. West (bottom); **Page 33:** Library of Congress (full page), Ronn Palm (inset); **Page 34:** The University of Texas at Auburn Eugene C. Barker Texas History Center (left), Library of Congress (top right), National Archives (inset); **Page 35:** New-York Historical Society; **Pages 36 and 37:** United States Army Military History Institute; **Page 38:** Library of Congress (bottom), Mississippi Department of Archives and History (inset); **Page 40:** William Turner (top), Historical Society of Missouri (inset); **Page 41:** *Harper's New Monthly,* July 1871 (top), United States Army Military History Institute (bottom); **Pages 42 through 44:** United States Army Military History Institute; **Page 45:** *Harper's New Monthly,* June 1857; **Page 46:** George Olinger Collection, Gettysburg (top two), National Archives (bottom); **Page 47:** United States Army Military History Institute (top), Library of Congress (bottom); **Page 48:** United States Army Military History Institute (top),

Harper's New Monthly, September 1861; **Page 49:** United States Army Military History Institute; **Page 50:** *Civil War Times;* **Page 51:** New-York Historical Society; **Page 52:** Library of Congress; **Page 53:** United States Army Military History Institute (left), Herb Peck, Jr. (right); **Page 54:** United States Army Military History Institute (top), Western Reserve Historical Society (inset); **Page 55:** Chicago Historical Society; **Page 56:** *Civil War Times;* **Page 58:** Neikrug Photographica, Ltd.; **Page 59:** Illinois State Historical Library; **Page 61:** Library of Congress.

~ QUOTATION CREDITS ~

Page 10: Ella Lonn, *Desertion during the Civil War,* p. 13.
Page 14: Walter Lowenfels, *Walt Whitman's Civil War,* pp. 21 and 22. **Page 17:** Paul Glass and Louis C. Singer, *Singing Soldiers,* pp. 106 and 107. **Page 18:** Louis P. Masur, *The Real War Will Never Get in the Books,* p. 78. **Page 20:** Edward L. Ayers, "A House Divided...", p. 128. **Page 23:** Glass and Singer, pp. 152 and 153. **Page 24:** Ayers, p. 40. **Page 26:** Ayers, p. 165.
Page 28: John Bartlett, *Bartlett's Familiar Quotations,* p. 440.
Page 32: Bob Zeller, *The Civil War in Depth,* p. 91.
Page 34: Patricia Faust, *Historical Times Illustrated Encyclopedia of the Civil War,* p. 74. **Page 36:** Masur, p. 80. **Page 38:** Ayers, pp. 155 and 156. **Page 40:** William R. Trotter, *Bushwhackers,* p. 200.
Page 41: Daniel E. Sutherland, *The Expansion of Everyday Life, 1860-1876,* p. 134. **Page 43:** Ayers, p. 126. **Page 45:** FitzGerald Ross, *Cities and Camps of the Confederate States,* p. 190.
Page 48: Ruth Scarborough, *Belle Boyd,* p. 145. **Page 51:** Darryl

Lyman, *Civil War Quotations*, p. 158. **Page 53:** Frederick Douglas, *Autobiographies*, p. 140. **Page 54:** Bartlett, p. 480. **Page 57:** Masur, p. 232. **Page 58:** Ayers, p. 164. **Page 60:** Peter G. Tsouras, *Military Quotations from the Civil War*, p. 125.

⁓ SELECT BIBLIOGRAPHY ⁓

Ayers, Edward L., ed. *"A House Divided...": A Century of Civil War Quotations*. New York: John Wiley and Sons, 1997.

Bartlett, John. *Bartlett's Familiar Quotations*. 16th edition. Edited by Justin Kaplan. Boston: Little, Brown, 1992.

Boatner, Mark M., III, *The Civil War Dictionary*. Revised edition. New York: Vintage Books, 1991.

Davis, William C., and Bell I. Wiley, eds. *Photographic History of the Civil War*. Reprint. 2 vols. New York: Black Dog and Leventhal, 1994.

Davis, William C., ed. *Touched by Fire: A Photographic Portrait of the Civil War*. 2 vols. Boston: Little, Brown, 1985.

Douglass, Frederick. *Autobiographies*. Reprint. New York: Library of America, 1994.

Faragher, John Mack, ed. *The American Heritage Encyclopedia of American History*. New York: Henry Holt, 1998.

Faust, Patricia, ed. *Historical Times Illustrated Encyclopedia of the Civil War*. New York: Harper and Row, 1986.

Frazier, Charles. *Cold Mountain*. New York: Atlantic Monthly Press, 1997.

Glass, Paul, and Louis C. Singer. *Singing Soldiers: A History of the Civil War in Song*. 1968. Reprint. New York: Da Capo Press, 1975.

Gragg, Rod, ed. *The Illustrated Confederate Reader*. New York: Harper and Row, 1989.

Kennedy, Frances H., ed. *The Civil War Battlefield Guide*. 2nd edition. New York: Houghton Mifflin, 1998.

Leisch, Juanita. *An Introduction to Civil War Civilians*. Gettysburg: Thomas, 1994.

Lonn, Ella. *Desertion during the Civil War*. 1928. Reprint. Lincoln: University of Nebraska Press, Bison Books, 1998.

Lowenfels, Walter, ed. *Walt Whitman's Civil War*. 1960. Reprint. New York: Da Capo Press.

Lyman, Darryl, ed. *Civil War Quotations*. Conshohocken, Pa.: Combined Books, 1995.

Masur, Louis P., ed. *The Real War Will Never Get in the Books: Selections from Writings during the Civil War*. New York: Oxford University Press, 1993.

McPherson, James M. *Battle Cry of Freedom: The Civil War Era*. New York: Oxford University Press, 1988.

Plante, Ellen M. *Women at Home in Victorian America: A Social History*. New York: Facts on File, 1997.

Ross, FitzGerald. *Cities and Camps of the Confederate States*. Reprint. Edited by Richard Barksdale Harwell. Chicago: University of Illinois Press, Illini Books, 1997.

Scarborough, Ruth. *Belle Boyd: Siren of the South*. 1984. Reprint. Macon: Mercer University Press, 1997.

Sutherland, Daniel E. *The Expansion of Everyday Life, 1860-1876*. New York: Harper and Row, 1989.

Trotter, William R. *Bushwhackers: The Civil War in North Carolina—The Mountains*. Winston-Salem: John F. Blair, 1988.

Tsouras, Peter J. *Military Quotations of the Civil War*. New York: Sterling, 1998.

Zeller, Bob. *The Civil War in Depth: History in 3-D*. San Francisco: Chronicle Books, 1997.